LET EVERYTHING COME TO YOU

True Stories That Have Helped Change Lives

MAURICE FULLARD SMITH

with

BRIDGET BOYLE

By the Author of 'THIS IS IT – The Art of Happily Going Nowhere'

LET EVERYTHING COME TO YOU

ISBN-13: 978-1541322677
ISBN-10: 1541322673

THANK YOU

Independent publishing, I said I would never do, but I recently decided to give myself a 90th birthday present by producing a little book for old friends who may well have heard these stories many times before.

This book could not have been presented without my dear friend Bridget Boyle who edited the manuscript, advised an elderly and at times confused technophobe wrestling to come to terms with a medium that he has never comprehended, and generally poured oil on troubled waters.

Eldest son, Dave, who gave willing hours of his time helping me get back online and up-to-speed broadband, after I had enjoyed some restful years free of Information Technology.

A surprise visit from my old friend Derrick Phillips brought a generous offer to publish on my behalf.

How good can people keep being to me?

To each I give my heartfelt thanks.

Contents

FOREWORD by Alan Halden

(friend and mentor)

This little book is humorous and honest. It is written with warmth and humanity about ordinary people in ordinary settings, helping us to find truth in unexpected places.

For Maurice Fullard Smith, truth is a quest not a definition. He does not understand truth as a word game, but as *the reality behind appearances.* He is remembered, by all who know him, as a storyteller, and so follows a tradition which goes back beyond the written word and which is the precursor of all literature.

Like all good raconteurs his anecdotes are not just entertaining, although they are certainly that, but leave the reader with a sense of somehow touching the inner kernel of life, of reality . . . of Truth.

INTRODUCTION

This little book of experiences is offered to help us see through to the truth of things rather than being dominated by what they appear to be on the surface. Very often a better word for truth is *reality*. What is the reality in all the experiences we have and often feel so intensely? Are we understanding what people mean, rather than just hearing their inadequate words? If we go through life judging only by surface appearances we shall often despair – but not so if, somehow, we catch a glimpse of the fact that our experiences, some of which we may hate, can in reality be working for us and transforming us.

This is especially so if we learn not to look at the things which are seen – that is the things that are tangibly obvious – but at the things which are at first unseen.

If you have realised that in the current maelstrom of hectic, performance-orientated living there is a need for calm and inner stillness, then this book is probably for you. If you have persevered, to the best of your ability, to follow techniques and methods toward this end, yet without satisfactory progress, then this book is even more for you. For I am one of your number, having given my all over several years and yet finding it was still not enough.

Evidently there is a basic deficiency somewhere. Why are some apparently able to find inner stillness, consciousness, a sense of presence and identity, a place of rest and satisfaction – not to mention being quietly confident throughout their lives – while the majority of us struggle from one author to another, one teaching to another, one religion to another, without a discovery that enables everyday living to be what we instinctively know it should be?

Before I attempt an answer, I want to say that if I were in your shoes right now I would probably be thinking, 'Oh, you're the only one with *the* answer, are you?' But hold on just a minute. My answer to that unspoken question is: 'No, I am not saying that at all, but I may be able to help a little.'

Yielding to the seemingly inevitable in our life situations we often find – although maybe only afterwards – that the pressures we are under can be good things, developing and enriching us so that we become fuller and more mature. Such a fact may seem quite impossible to many at this moment, but multitudes have proved it to be true; once they had learned to *be just here now*, without constantly fighting their circumstances.

Now I don't want you to get the idea that this is a book slanted towards some dreadful stoicism; rather, I trust it will be light-hearted and not add any further burdens to your life, for there are plenty around already.

My fervent hope is that, as you read on, you will increasingly see through all the problems that we face in these early years of the 21st century and discover something of a blissful eternal reality, the hidden Mystery which we can explore to great benefit even though we shall never fully understand with our finite minds the infinite majesty of the incredible universe. I also hope you will capture something of the stillness that has come into my own life in latter years.

I wish you happy and relaxed reading as I retell some of my experiences, which were not in essence what they at first appeared to be. Hopefully I can now increasingly leave all these stories in the past and live more fully in this present moment, which is the wonderful secret of true living, unknown to so many of us for so long. Meanwhile, I have found the stories often seem to touch the latent inner wellspring of many people, bringing acceptance and peace.

EXPLORING THE MYSTERY

We were in London's theatreland. My wife and I had just witnessed the final scene of The Mousetrap, the record-breaking play by Agatha Christie. (It's still running and in its 60th year as I write!) We had sat through two hours of mystery.

Once we had learned 'whodunit' a member of the cast stepped through the centre curtains and asked us not to tell our friends, not to spoil their enjoyment – perhaps also not to affect future attendances and profit.

As we mounted the stairs in the circle to leave the building I noticed an atmosphere quite different from the normal chatter that follows many theatre performances. Hundreds of people were making a rather hushed exit together. My wife had not noticed this until I pointed it out, but then I have always been ultra-sensitive to atmosphere. 'You're right,' she said, 'it *is* different'.

Things quickly returned to normal once we emerged on to the West End street, but mulling the matter over as we walked I soon realised what had happened. We had all shared in a sense of mystery, a secret finally revealed. There was a sense of the esoteric. Somehow, we were all held quietly together; to say we had bated breath would be an exaggeration, but it came close to it.

This is how I understand spiritual truth or reality to be; a series of discoveries that deeply affects us and give us a sense of wonder. However, it seems to me we shall never fully understand this amazing life; the sense of mystery will always be there. In fact, as we progress it will probably increase. The more we know, the more we shall realise there is to know. Perhaps like learned astronomers whose every discovery leads to an even greater unfathomable dimension.

Life is not a problem to be solved but a mystery to be explored, as a friend of mine once gently informed me. I liked that. It could be trite and unkind to say glibly that all our problems are hidden opportunities, for many of life's experiences are long, painful, and extremely distressing.

Yet I believe there is truth within that statement, though it may not always be prudent to say so.

Those who assert they have 'solved the problem' of truth once and for all, those for whom all the evidence is in, never experience a continuing sense of unfolding wonder. However real our initial conscious encounter with reality may be, we need an ongoing sense of exploration to know the constant presence of the quiet thrill of living. I am not referring to the intensity of a frantic search, but to an openness to discovery until the last moment of our lives. The facing of all we encounter with as much honesty as possible.

Surely even the hereafter will be just another step into the unknown, into the wonder of discovery, albeit a colossal step and one which every one of us must eventually take. Death remains a mystery, no matter how sure we may feel of our destiny. And somehow I am strangely glad it does. Even J.M. Barrie's Peter Pan envisaged dying with a slight frisson of excitement, musing that "To die will be an awfully big Adventure."

Don't fear the unknown – enjoy the mystery

SUNRISE ON EVEREST

It was too breathtaking for him even to gasp, 'Wow!'

It is many years since the eloquent Indian speaker Bakt Singh came to London and I heard a true story that helped to redirect my life radically.

He told us how he had always longed to see the sunrise on Mount Everest, in fact ever since a friend had eulogised about the sight. One day while travelling in the Himalayas he got the opportunity, but of course it meant getting up in the middle of the night. Along with a dozen others he was led by a Sherpa guide to the viewing point. The group stood quietly together in the darkness as the sun gradually rose and they could see Everest away in the distance.

After a short while, one by one the party started to turn and make their way down the hillside, but Bakt Singh remained.

He turned to the guide and said he was not very impressed with the sight; it was nowhere near as wonderful as he had been led to believe.

'Stand still, sahib' replied the guide, 'and wait until the mist clears away'.

The pair stood alone gazing into the distance while the rest walked back down the hill commenting on the sight they had witnessed. Maybe they were professional tourists and just wanted to tell their friends where they had been; it was obviously not essential to them for the goods to match the advertising. They had seen the event and that was enough. They would tell all their friends that they had indeed seen the sunrise on Mount Everest. They were not liars, what they said was true, but it was not the truth. They didn't even realise there was more.

Bakt Singh waited in the stillness as the mists gradually cleared. He said it was as if the world's highest mountain leaped from the background to the foreground and stood just before him in glorious majesty. 'I felt I could almost reach out and touch the summit,' he whispered.

The others had seen the day break on Everest, but they not had the same experience as Bakt Singh. He would never forget, never need to exaggerate. He had seen the living reality and received an awesome and indelible impression, an imprint on his soul.

For many years, I had sensed that in terms of spiritual experience and understanding there must be more; we do not have to settle for the same experience as everyone else. But if we can be honest about the reality of our own experience and then, with a calm awareness, just wait for the mists to clear of their own accord, more wonders will be unveiled. Bakt Singh helped me begin to understand this and increased my desire to know more of the mystery that can be explored if we learn to be still and unhurried. The mists will clear. A breath-taking new vision will reveal itself.

The sun will not be hurried in burning off the mist

THE RACE OF LIFE

I was not very good at ball games and was usually left until near last when two captains picked their teams at school. Sports day wasn't much fun either because I could not sprint very fast and my eleven-year-old girlfriend was the Middlesex county champion for her age group.

However, one day I received third prize in the sixty yards dash. Instead of liberating me into the realms of accepted young sportsmen, the prize-giving crippled me inside and made me ashamed. I had not come third; Joyce had elevated me from fifth, as she was the young judge chosen to watch for the third placed runner. She had cheated on my behalf.

Years later, during World War Two, I was called for military service. My posting was to an Infantry Training Battalion for potential leaders where platoon sergeants marched us to exhaustion and physical training instructors chased us over obstacle courses whilst bellowing insults in our ears.

'SMITH! … My grandmother can move faster than you!'

Came a hot summer day when the platoon lined up in full battle order – steel helmets, rifles, back-packs, heavy boots, the lot. The senior PTI barked, 'You'll run two miles down this road, round the telephone box on the village green and back. Fast as you can: MOO-OOVE !!!'

Once out of sight a few clever barrack-room lawyers climbed into a field ready to join in when we came back. It was not long before I began to wonder what was wrong with everyone, for the further we went the easier I found it to stay in front. From behind the halfway telephone box a crafty sergeant stepped out to rubber stamp the palms of our hands, to prove we had run the full course. It was rewarding to display this when the lads optimistically jumped back on to the tarmac to join me in the lead. The last I saw they were heading off in the opposite direction.

As I reached the barracks the familiar red and black striped jerseys of the Physical Training Instructors were plain to see. I was a clear winner and prepared myself to receive their congratulations. They were obviously surprised to see who was in front.

'*Thank God you can do something, Smith!*' bawled the hated senior instructor.

I was hitherto unaware of his interest in the Almighty, but the insult didn't matter. The reality was I could run long distances without distress. Out-run by granny? Not true! I wasn't slower than his grandmother. Nothing could rob me of my surprise achievement. I hadn't cheated this time. I can only say I felt liberated; the reality had set me free. I had discovered what hitherto had been locked up inside me and my gift had been released. I could run fast for long distances and had found my hobby for a lifetime.

Over sixty years later I have learned that our worth does not depend upon our abilities. We are all unique, valuable, and acceptable without having to attain. It is participating in life that matters, not just winning. There is more locked away inside us than we have ever realised, we are all intrinsically wonderful and every single one has some special gift to contribute to the whole.

I first wrote this article on day one of the Sydney Olympic Games in the year 2000 and I wonder how many of the athletes had such an attitude? Taking part, not just winning, is the sentiment expressed in the Olympic motto.

Sadly, winning has become nearly everything and for many the motto is 'Second is nowhere.' What a tragedy. And it is not true. The trouble with coming first is that it is necessarily at the expense of all the others who don't; there is always a sense of derogatory sneering about the term 'also-ran.' Thankfully, I have finally learned the truth that is the joy of participation and am glad just to be a runner in the race of life where we can all be true winners, and at nobody else's expense.

'To your marks . . .'

YOU don't have to be good at what THEY are good at

SEEING WITH THE HEART

Spiritual truth is not really a matter of information, but of revelation. *Truth* needs to be *seen.* Information may be an accurate forerunner, but it is not necessarily of much help. Even Albert Einstein said, 'The only thing that interferes with my learning is my education.' It's not formal instruction that counts, it is what you get to find out that matters.

Imagine this scene from childhood – so many years ago that the detail is probably now only loosely accurate. A friendly Primary School teacher leaned over my desk to help me with a problem. We had small classes in those days and I was usually at the bottom of the class for arithmetic, or 'sums' as we called the subject then. In that pre-computer age, we worked with a little abacus and I can remember the lady teacher moving the beads along . . . two and two . . . three and one . . . two and one and one.

Each time a different combination added up to the same total and I was well confused.

Eventually after much personal tuition and perseverance on her part, the light dawned and I was really excited. 'Oh . . . I *see!*' I shrilled with obvious joy (well it was something like that). The penny had finally dropped.

Actually, I had 'understood', but that would not have adequately described what had happened inside me. There had been an inner illumination and what I had seen I would never un-see. I can still add well. That small incident made a lasting impression on me. I am only this moment realising that blind people also use the expression, "I see!" They are seeing with inner eyes and that's what I am talking about.

Jesus is reported to have asked one of his followers, 'Who do you say that I am?' When Peter exclaimed, 'You are the Christ . . . you're the son of the living God!' he wasn't making a factual statement so much as saying, "Oh, I see! *That's* who you are!" Because suddenly he'd got it! The penny had dropped.

It would be this realisation, the reality of his understanding that would enable Peter to cope with all his future trials, both his successes and his failures, not some mental assent to a fact.

This inner truth would have a firm grip on him and constantly change his life.

This is true in everyday life. If we take note of all the information and every imperative or exhortation we hear and read, regardless of whether it lights up within us or not, then we shall soon be in deep trouble. A crushing and debilitating sense of guilt will quickly head our way as we struggle to attain without any inner dynamic to enable us to succeed.

Information and application are useful for mathematicians no doubt, but only up to a point. There comes a stage where they are not enough, as Einstein did not shrink from pointing out. These attributes alone are inadequate for spiritual endeavour or a satisfied life. Little wonder I only take serious note of, and act upon, the things that light up to me. I have learned the hard way that the 'The letter kills, but the spirit gives life.' Literal nit-picking adherence is flat and dead, but the spirit energises and motivates. Naturally I have been accused of picking and choosing only what appeals to me, but I can cope with that.

Much of what we know needs an eighteen-inch drop from the head to the heart, for our spiritual eyes are in our heart.

We need to be less obsessed with accuracy. As John Wesley observed, truth must *touch* us so that we are 'strangely moved,' then it becomes a living reality affecting our daily lives. And that's the nub of it!

"With the eyes of your hearts enlightened, you will know the confidence that comes from God having called you." - St Paul

STILLNESS IS NOT DIFFICULT

Since writing my last book 'This Is It' I have been bombarded with enthusiastic congratulations on its simplicity and readability. Spiritually-minded folk can understand the benefits of living in this moment, enjoying internal stillness, not being ruled by a restless mind or overactive imagination. I have been equally assailed by those who say they just cannot do it and this has distressed me.

I'm annoyed with myself that I cannot put it any more clearly that we never get into a more still, moment by moment experience by making an effort. It is an ever-present gift waiting for us to discover. Maybe it will help a little if I blurt out, as I do when public speaking:

> 'For most of us becoming still is not difficult - it is impossible!'

For many of us accepting this statement is only possible when we have striven until we are exhausted, until we cannot try any more, until in fact:

. . . stillness comes.

Attaining stillness inside is far easier for people from the Eastern hemisphere where activity of the right-hand side of the brain is valued as highly as that of the left, maybe even more so. Here in the west we have almost idolised logic and the scientific approach, in fact, all the very necessary attributes supplied by the left part of the brain. To be intuitive is generally to be held in suspicion and the artistic or creative temperament is often a cause for disdain, or damned with faint praise, especially by those whose main aim is life is to get on, make money, to attain power or prestige in a grossly materialistic and technical society. Instant gratification is the enemy of just being still. The amazing way the East is now developing suggests it will not be long before few there can enjoy the rich inner heritage which for many was once the natural inheritance from their forbears, and their early years around restful parents.

Unfortunately, even that which should come naturally to those with the right genes and upbringing has become systematised with the increasing advent of professional meditation gurus. That which should be a simple and pleasant pathway has become one of stringent discipline, attractive only to those who have a particular temperament.

But where I have encountered the products of such intensive methods, I have not usually enjoyed relaxed company in everyday life. Rather, I have seen an intense sense of imposed control and often a kind of pseudo-spirituality and sometimes even superiority. To a point, these methods may work in a low-key organised course or workshop (such as many yoga groups), and can be very beneficial to the physical health of the participants, but they do not provide the ongoing sense of inner stillness that many of us desire for our daily lives. Doubtless there are exceptions to the opinions I have expressed, as the gracious writings of some current authors have confirmed to me.

Most of us believe that everything has to be earned, and that rewards only come with hard work. In my early days this was known as the Protestant Work Ethic, where instead of following the desires springing up within us, we were urged to go against the natural flow of our temperament and feelings, which have always been suspect in our western culture.

This is in spite of constantly expressed clichéd statements such as 'go with the flow,' 'stay cool' and 'hang loose.' These are beneficial attributes that cannot just be stuck on the outside of our temperament and personality, or entrenched through discipline. True as they are, they need an inner spark or a change of mindset. Something organic has to happen. One might almost say that in this age, a revelation is needed, an inner illumination or enlightenment. And to use a hackneyed phrase, this is 'more often caught than taught.' Meeting someone with inner calm and quietude often has a quickening effect within us, and more exposure may cause us to also begin to relax. Inner calm, or we could even say bliss, does not require application so much as relaxation.

Perhaps we should leave matters there for the moment. Before proceeding it would be good to realise that just memorising this content will not help. It needs to be breathed into us.

'Information needs to become revelation' may seem a rather simplistic slogan but it is a favourite saying of mine, so to aid this I would encourage you to take a physical breather, perhaps just slump down where you are and remain silent for a while.

No pressure, do it only if you want to; but I have found that frequent pausing, perhaps sighing and relaxing every part of our bodies, is a great help and becomes a regular pleasing habit, but not a discipline. No trying mind you, just be where and as you are, and let go.

Be still in the presence of the LORD, and wait patiently for him to act - Psalm 37

THE RING OF TRUTH

A speaker came to England from abroad and was about to embark on a tour where he was conducting motivational meetings in people's homes. The moment I met this man my inner warning bells began to ring. There was something impure about him. I could produce no evidence of past misdemeanours and was talked down by my peers. In fact I was severely criticised for saying that I could not trust this man. 'What *evidence* did I have?' It subsequently turned out that he seduced several women while their husbands were at work. After that disaster one prominent and respected man said, 'We must ask Maurice what he feels in future.' But usually they did not; that would have been far too subjective.

The writer J.B. Phillips made a deep impression on me. His book was called 'The Ring of Truth' and that title has stayed in my consciousness ever since. Sometimes when listening to a narrative we sense, 'This doesn't ring true.'

Such an uncertain feeling can fly in the face of the evidence and tell us that something is wrong. Alternatively, a most unlikely story can carry a strange sense of authenticity, which goes beyond reason. Court witnesses may give seemingly contradictory accounts of an incident from their differing viewpoints but nonetheless, a good jury will discern the chime, the resonance of truth beneath any posturing. In the western world we have tended to base all our conclusions on logic and scientific evidence alone and have ignored our innermost feelings. In so doing we have lost a great deal.

Consider the forbidding term, used in some Church, Mosque, Synagogue, Temple or other didactic learning circles: 'Sound Teaching'. At face value it has a heavy, rather grave and prohibitive sound about it, possibly indicating a pernickety emphasis upon accuracy. But such may be far from a full understanding. How about 'sound' as in healthy? 'Sound in wind and limb' makes a good racehorse. An apple can be sound and very health-bestowing too.

Now we are beginning to focus! For a teaching, a philosophy or an ethic to be 'sound' it must bring nothing that can cause harm or dis-ease; healthy teaching or counsel is life-giving, containing no words to corrupt us or curtail our joy. In the same way that we listen to a bell that has a 'sound' or uncracked ring to it and gives us pleasure, so we should listen to the words we hear or read, because how something rings our bell can be the test for survival in certain circumstances. We relegate or ignore the ring of truth or untruth at our peril.

This is well illustrated by a woman who says she does not like being left alone in the house with a certain man. Often the response from her partner will be that she should stop being foolish. However, she may be picking up bad vibes or an uncertain sound or feeling – a flaw in the *ring* that is not easily explained. It is important that we learn to listen to what we hear deep inside ourselves, what many would call a 'gut feeling'. Of course it is risky and we may make some mistakes, because we are untrained and for far too long have ignored the still small voice inside.

When our inner umpire is calling 'Out!' we should start to take notice and make haste slowly. I have ridden roughshod over that inner registration too many times and paid a very high price. Now I am learning to listen increasingly for the ring of reality – to be sure the sound of that whistle came from the referee and not from the crowd. If I learn this well then I shall suffer fewer unnecessary wounds in future.

In the natural world, this happens easily. Animals rely upon it. We call it instinct. Did I say *IN the natural world?* How strange that we should feel ourselves to be outside the natural world, not part of it, not natural! A leopard – and for that matter, an antelope – puts its total trust in the inner voice of instinct. Instinct is that inherent insight, the deep inner knowledge of how to interpret and react to all that the leopard watches, hears, senses and is aware of. Minute by minute in the antelope's daily life, its ongoing security and well-being depend upon its unswerving confidence in that instinct, that inner voice that deeply *knows.*

Once again we are discovering that things are often not what they appear to be.

If we refrain from using only our 'rational' minds to pass judgement on every person, statement or happenstance, we open ourselves to the deep impression of reality that is present at all times, ready to ease our way through life. It's not a case of letting your heart rule your head – you have to go deeper than that; trust your instinct.

Trust yourself. You know more than you think you do - Dr Benjamin Spock

SINGING IN THE RAIN

'It's a foul day, Nick,' I sighed heavily as we drove towards a speaking engagement in South London. 'It is raining hard' he replied, 'But I enjoy the rain.'

That poignant remark made over thirty years ago opened up a whole new avenue of thought to me. I realised that if upon waking I found the sun shining brightly, I got off to a much better start. It occurred to me that I had been walking through life with my eyes half-closed. Unless the scene was one of extreme and immediate impact I was switched off and could be missing quite a lot.

I had to admit to very little appreciation of the varied creation around me. In order to see and experience more of this reality it would be necessary to begin to open my eyes and become aware of a whole new world of variety and subtlety. The opportunity soon came.

Eileen and I took a much-needed winter break in the Peak District. We booked into a comfortable hotel and were looking forward to some time together away from our responsibilities.

The sun was shining as we left Essex on the Friday afternoon, which was unusual for mid-January. We cheerfully headed north towards the scenic delights of Derbyshire.

Arriving earlier than anticipated we exploited the unexpected bonus of a few hours of weak winter sunshine by exploring the local dales and watercourses. They were both beautiful and exhilarating. We continued enjoying the scenery until darkness fully descended and then returned to our hotel for a splendid meal before retiring to bed in jubilant mood. All was going well.

At about one o'clock I turned over in bed and was forced to acknowledge that the noise I could hear was torrential rain. I clambered out of bed, closed the window and then curled up again with a groan and went back to sleep.

Morning brought no respite, for the day was wet and grey. I very nearly slipped into my routine way of thinking, which would have meant retreating to a corner of the lounge to bury my nose in a book for the day. But we could do that at home!

Then I remembered that Nick said he enjoyed the rain, that life is not all spectacular sunrises and sunsets, there is a whole world of subtle variety to be appreciated, but enjoying it takes a little more application. You have to be at peace with yourself to notice it, for subtlety is not always immediately rewarding. We miss this if we demand instant gratification.

So we decided on the hills. While some of the other guests huddled into easy chairs, we climbed into the MG sports car, kindly loaned by a friend, and cautiously nosed our way out of the long driveway. The car interior soon misted up and I had to lower the window to clear it. In came a few spots of uninvited rain. Having experienced a slight change of attitude, I noticed that these raindrops were quite refreshing and now not at all unwelcome. As we pressed on, dark cloud formations drew our attention to the ever-changing pattern of the sky. I realised for the first time in my life that grey was not *just* grey; there were different shades of grey. Until then I had felt grey was a colour we could well do without – and today it is still not among my favourites.

Suddenly the wind whipped up and swept the clouds rapidly across our vision. The rain stopped for a moment and a tantalising snatch of blue sky opened up, seemingly full of promise. I found myself absorbed in the world of natural creation in quite a new way. I was certainly more at peace than usual, as I would normally have been indulging in continual complaints about the foul British weather and our ruined weekend. We were genuinely happy, even as we watched the patch of blue disappear and were plunged once more into heavy cloud.

Before our forty-eight hours were over we had experienced a crash course in the elements. Rain, sun and wind, even a smattering of sleet for good measure. What a great weekend it was, when it could have been a miserable disappointment if my thinking had remained unchanged. Everything had been much better than it seemed it would be when I awoke to hear the pouring rain during our first night away. This was another positive step along the road for me, realising that life was not meant to be always full of intensely satisfying purpose and heart-stopping beauty. That would never be the reality.

There would be dark times to contrast the happy times, and bland ordinary periods, perhaps as a backdrop to the more exotic times we experience, but these seemingly dull and flat times are not to be ignored. Every moment and every situation is part of the fabric of life to be consciously entered into. No need to run from unpleasant experiences and painful circumstances. They may be too dire to be enjoyed, but they play their part in the development of a full-orbed life.

I used to plead constantly with a Higher Power to change things for the apparent better, but as these pages reveal, it is taking a lifetime to become a master in the art of living in each moment, exactly as it comes.

"The past has no power over the present moment. ... It is as it is." Eckhart Tolle

INTUITION IN PRAGUE

The Iron Curtain had done its best to shut out western enthusiasts, but we were quite young and adventurous. Before long we had discovered fellow spiritually-minded people in several communist countries and were making clandestine visits behind the Iron Curtain with money and literature. We were invited to speak at one of their many secret underground rendezvous.

Now, in my later mid-eighties, my deep sense of unity with the Eternal Presence is stronger than ever, but I now recognise that Presence within a far broader context and having a far wider interpretation than I did then. At that time I recognised a sense of the divine, and saw the expression of that Timeless Unity, only in terms of Christianity.

My spiritual insights were deep, genuine and at times quite overwhelming, but I didn't realise that this enlightenment was only from one perspective. In these later years I acknowledge that all matters of life - of body, soul and spirit - are far more harmoniously fused than I ever imagined.

In those days my vision of the love, power and purpose of the Universe involved only one name, and that for me was Jesus. That was the name under which until then all my spiritual experience had come to me. For others the moment their lights came on may well have been an encounter with the Krishna, Buddha, Allah, or none of the above. What an expansion that has been.

So back to my story. I was a regular Christian speaker and this one night I had been speaking to an 'underground' group of young people; literally under the ground in a basement in Prague.

They were quite evidently stirred by my message and I could see they would have a new resolve to be bold in their difficult and hostile environment. Once I had finished the elderly pastor rose purposefully to his feet and spoke very seriously. My interpreter whispered to me that he was warning everyone to ignore what I had said as their obvious excitement could lead to persecution and imprisonment. It was all right for me, he said, I would soon be returning to safety in England and to the unhindered comfort of my wife and children.

Things were different under their regime, he reminded them. That hadn't occurred to me, but now older and wiser I can understand his concern for those headstrong young people.

The next day I was walking the streets of Prague feeling a little depressed that my efforts had been so frustrated, concerned that the cautious older man had put such a dampener on the spiritual fire which had been ignited. But what could I do, I had such a language limitation?

An imposing building caught my eye and I had a strange feeling I should go inside. After a moment's hesitation I crossed the road, climbed the steps and pushed open the door. To my surprise I found it was a library.

As I walked among all the books, the words of which I could not understand, I was puzzled and wondering why I had followed my intuition. Then I spotted a notice that read *English Section.* Tucked away in a corner there were a few lonely books under the further heading of *The Mystics.*

I reached up and randomly picked out one of the books. Opening at the frontispiece I saw a few words written in large, bold print:

- Some hounds run because they have seen the hare,
- Some hounds run because the other hounds are running.

In an instant I was at peace. I returned the book and strode away. There was nothing to worry about. If those young people had caught sight of the Reality I was enthusing about, they would be OK. They would last the course. Nothing would deter them from following the light that they had seen – and probably do so a little more wisely after the exhortation from their elder statesman.

I was so glad I had responded to that inner impulse, that gentle intuitive pull that had drawn me into a foreign library. I had discovered a further glimpse of reality in a profound couplet I would never forget – one that in future years would affect the lives of many more people as I told the story again and again in different countries. The visit to Prague was not a wasted visit after all. It was more than it seemed in my hasty conclusion after the meeting, and maybe some of those young people are still feeling the benefit today, who knows?

It is through science that we prove, but through intuition that we discover.

Henri Poincaré, mathematician and physicist

LED BY A LITTLE CHILD

A little child introduced me to the Magic Eye books.

The pages of these books contain intricate printed patterns which, although intriguing in themselves, when stared at with *eyes leisurely focused just beyond the surface of the page,* they each reveal a hidden secret. If we develop stillness and the ability to relax, we can look beyond the obvious outward appearance and something magical happens. The pictures are suddenly revealed as three-dimensional and are often very beautiful. Life is like that.

Over-concentration is a great hindrance, but while some concentrate too hard, others are content with just a surface glance. Through neither approach will you experience the hidden revelations that at times can be quite staggering. Calmly focusing, miracles can happen. Thankfully, being a bit of a dreamer, I can usually 'see through' and experience what some others, for all their intensity, cannot see.

Truth is the reality that lies beyond the surface appearance.

When Jesus said 'I am the truth,' he was not claiming to be the ultimate embodiment of accurate doctrine or dogma, rather that he had discovered the key to the very essence of all Being, inside himself. That can happen to us and is doing so in this age more and more.

True information may be found in many writings and many places but inner truth is not to be found lying carelessly around on the surface of the pages of a holy book – Torah, Bible, Koran, Bhagavad-Gita or any other – nor in a religious building *per se*; although it may be discovered in any one of these, or a million other places, everywhere. It is the unveiling of the heart of the Divinity who is hidden in human flesh and blood, even today. When we are at rest from striving and can recognise our own deepest being, at one with every living thing, then every one of us is able to say, 'I am the truth.'

But we have to become as a little child to see that.

"Become like a little child" - Jesus of Nazareth

PACE KILLS – NEVER DISTANCE

The scene was our local petrol station forecourt and, for a surprise, the automatic car wash was in working order. Not only in working order but devoid of the line of cars so often there to test my patience. Not one single car in sight. Parking by the pay office, I obtained my token and eagerly drove round to the washing machine entrance. What's this? Another car has slipped in before me? Not only that, there is no driver in it, only his wife and children. I began to fret.

The better part of me whispered, '*Calm down Maurice, you're in no hurry. You can sit back and enjoy your John Williams tape.*' So I leaned back and enjoyed the music. Of course this is better. What's the urgency anyway? Two minutes later – Where on earth is the man?

'Keep calm. Rest back. It is minutes we are on about, not hours'.

Oh yes, sorry I forgot; I expect he's parked first and gone for his token . . . what am I saying? Parked first? That is not fair!

I'll have a word with his wife (politely of course) then look for the man himself. What does he think he's up to? I was here first!

All the while a small still voice inside was persisting, *'Cool it, Maurice, cool it!'* But my adrenalin was now pumping and breaking through my peace barrier. I jumped out of the car leaving the engine running and the automatic selector column safely in neutral. I guess I must have closed the door rather heavily (slammed is such an aggressive word) because although the car was stationary as I got out, while I was talking to the lady in front I turned to see it moving at considerable speed in reverse. The door was still shut and there was no one inside.

I panicked and chased furiously after the phantom vehicle, quickly realising by the increasing speed that the manual choke was still out. I failed to reach the monster before it charged through a ten-foot high fence and came to rest against a lorry wheel in the adjoining car park. There it stood with all but the back end protruding defiantly from the jagged opening.

Oh my! This wasn't going to look good on the accident report and I didn't relish my explanation to the filling-station owner either.

Standing there inspecting the crumpled rear end and the shattered fencing, I momentarily wondered if it would be a good idea to slip quietly away.

I would need to phone the insurance brokers too. Oh my goodness – I'd only had the car a month and they were already involved trying to settle a claim for an incident when I had misjudged my distance and dented the *front* end coming out of a multi-storey car park. I realised this was going to ruin my no-claims bonus. Recent thoughts of taking an Advanced Drivers' test were relegated by about twenty-five years. Self-pity set in. Maybe I should give up driving? Or emigrate!

The moral of this story is: never leave an automatic car with the engine running, it could shudder into gear and take off . . .

"No, it isn't Maurice! The moral is: Listen to your inner spirit whispering that patience is a virtue. I'd like you to stop fretting and fussing, to realise that life cannot be rushed. It is a marathon not a sprint. As I said, 'Enjoy your John Williams music.'"

It may seem to some of us that we'll do better by always hurrying things along, but it is far from the truth. Of course, in this instance, things could have been far worse.

The car could have hit and injured someone. It was annoying, but not too expensive, except in terms of pride. Quite inexpensive really, if it began to teach me to 'slow down, you move to fast,' which ironically was the title of a song I was always singing around that time. A three-year-old little lady in Florida later emphatically pressed this advice home when she looked up at me and said boldly, word for word, *'Maurice, you move too fast!'*

I am slowing down, but gradually. 'Pace kills, never distance' is a well-known watchword for all good marathon runners and should be heeded by us all. We'll certainly 'hit the wall' if we don't.

"They stumble that run fast" – Shakespeare

GROWING TO MATURITY

Our lives hold a natural sense of progression. There is nothing wrong with living comfortably with ourselves at different stages of life. I am minded to say how sad it is that we have largely lost such an attitude, for our children are now urged to grow old prematurely with all the havoc and distress that ensues. Let them enjoy their childhood is a plea from my heart. It's also interesting that just as our young are not allowed to be children, in some respects our elderly are not allowed to grow old, either – "Dye your hair! Have a face-lift! But you're only 75yrs old, you should go back-packing across the Andes – don't dare sit down and admit you ache!"

The issue we are considering is that of maturity. Childhood is perfect for children. Continuing to live life as an infant who demands instant gratification has led to the crammed conditions in our penal institutions, ever replenished by those who are a law unto themselves, who have never been lovingly taught otherwise.

Believing the world revolves around our individual lives and that we can selfishly run our own show, leads to all kinds of childish 'mischief' that is not one bit endearing in the older adolescent. Pride certainly does precede a fall. I've been there!

Then there are the many idealistic young people, all too ready to fight the evils of the world, which cannot be a bad thing. They are so often instinctively aware of injustice and quickly conclude the solution is a simplistic battle between right and wrong. I spent many years clambering among the branches of 'the tree of the knowledge of good and evil' before I realised how inter-twined they are. I refer of course to the image of the two trees in the Garden of Eden, one 'The tree of the knowledge of good and evil,' the other 'the tree of Life.' The first one lives at best by weighing up pros and cons – more often by judging, labelling and criticising. The other lives by disregarding the seeming orthodoxies of right and wrong, asking only " – but does it *live?* Is there *life* in this instinct? Does this decision sit comfortably with my deepest true self?"

Increasing maturity eventually brings the peaceful understanding that, in spite of stark and terrible evidence to suggest otherwise, somehow everything is going to work out all right in the end. There is no big contest. There will be the happy ending we long for, but probably not the one we think is the best. Julian of Norwich's most famous utterance made many centuries ago rings again down the corridors of time, true as ever: 'All shall be well, and all shall be well, and all manner of thing shall be well.' Younger explorers of life find great encouragement and security in being around adults with such a firm and quiet assurance. However, history has taught us that such maturity does not come automatically with advancing years; we can become old and very foolish.

The truth is that each stage of a maturing life is OK for those involved. We need to realise there is something intrinsically *right* with us as we grow spiritually. In its early days it's entirely right that a developing apple is hard and green – and even sour!

Constantly emphasising mistakes and shortcomings, or trying to force-grow others to see our point of view, leads to a poor sense of self-worth. Sadly such an approach seems the main thrust of much religious activity.

A sense that we are all perfectly all right exactly as we are right now, though massively flawed, comes from the security that arises when we know we are loved and warmly forgiven. Unilateral forgiveness and total acceptance mark the pathway to a willing malleability, or learning a responsible way to live.

If we step outside ourselves now and then, we may thankfully observe that we are growing up into a restful and sure knowledge that there is a heart and an intelligence in and behind all things. Perhaps a heart that is breaking? This constant all-pervading Spirit has been around from the beginning. It is remarkable how truly saintly people have discovered this truth in the turmoil of persecution and suffering. For this to happen we surely need to be mysteriously gripped by the sense of another dimension of reality, especially when we survey the unspeakable horror breaking out like an angry carcinoma across the whole of the modern world.

Even as I write these words I am consumed with personal family grief, but I am also undergirded by a sense of ultimate well-being. I know really that 'All shall be well,' even when it doesn't feel like it right now. And believe you me, it doesn't!

When peace like a river attendeth my way,
Or sorrows like sea billows roll …
… It is well, it is well, with my soul.
Horatio Spafford

USING OUR IMAGINATION

'Imagine!' urges John Lennon. A strong imagination is a wonderful gift, but one not possessed by all. Those who lack in this area seem to miss much of the excitement in life, yet are likely to be compensated by a much smoother ride.

My wife and I illustrate the point perfectly. Innumerable times I have said to her, 'This place is not how I imagined it. How about you?' Eileen's inevitable reply would be, 'I didn't think about it.' She waits until she gets there to see what a place is like. Although she lives in this present moment and seems to cope and largely enjoy what it brings, there is no savouring of the future and no disappointment on arrival. She does not demand much of life, makes an intelligent enquiry about anything she wants to know and is content.

So often the reverse has been true in my case.

When our holiday 'sports facilities' prove not to be a full scale fitness suite and an Olympic-size pool, but one small table-tennis table in a shed out the back of some farmhouse, then I regret having substituted a vivid imagination for an intelligent enquiry. Imagination can lead us to huge disappointment! That is not a serious application of this issue; but think of the pain caused by an undisciplined imagination whilst awaiting the results of a hospital scan, or speculating on the development of a serious illness in the case of a loved one. Imagination can lead us into anxiety, and outright fear.

Of course, insisting that we cease dwelling on morbid possibilities can be like telling a hungry child he can think of anything he wants to – except a good meal! Forbidding seems to increase the attraction. When my over-fertile imagination begins to run amok, leading me into the paths of Possible Dire Consequences, I know it is time to rest back, take a few deep breaths, indulge in a wry smile at past inaccuracies and return to the present moment.

'We don't *know* that, it may not be the whole truth of the matter,' I tell myself. Then, in my weakness, I lean back into the Conscious Presence who is my true inner life.

Years ago, I learned the truth that 'Of myself I can do nothing,' (to quote the reported words of Jesus) but now I am learning that everything is possible to those whose weakness is infused with divine strength. It is taking a painfully long time to perfect this understanding as will unfold in the following pages, but I am still learning – and may it ever be so.

You may object that a strong imagination is not necessarily a weakness and I would agree that it can be a tremendous asset, sparking off an inner creativity that brings satisfaction to ourselves and serves our fellows. 'I saw the angel in the marble and carved until I set him free,' said Michelangelo. However, I have also repeatedly found that our strengths can invariably become our weaknesses. In an independent self-confidence there is danger; we can easily go over the top. Armed with this foreknowledge we have nothing to fear as our imagination comes under control.

We can return peacefully to the inner truth now and not follow every outrageous thought. We shall most likely be led into a less dissipated state and be better equipped to deal with whatever happens in our life situation, which so often turns out to be very different from what our unruly imagination is telling us.

'Unruly' is the key word, perhaps. Imagination itself is neither good nor bad. Imagination is a neutral 'engine' that can be harnessed to generate distress or it can be employed to inspire! Muhammad Ali, whose imagination caused him to claim that he would 'float like a butterfly, sting like a bee,' maintained that 'the man who has no imagination has no wings.'

Imagine […

…] And no religion too

Imagine all the people living life in peace

John Lennon

ADVERSITY PLAYS ITS PART

I have worried in earnest for most of my life and I am not proud of it. Worrying has done inestimable harm to me both emotionally and physically, for the welfare of our mind and body is undoubtedly linked. Even though my repeatedly stressed condition caused considerable concern to those who loved me, I could not turn off the anxiety that was causing it.

The seeds of my condition are easily traced back to my illegitimate birth and to the environment of my early adoption by an elderly couple, who watched every move I made with great anxiety. As a very young child I can remember constant warnings of danger lurking everywhere. A trip to the swimming pool was likely to lead to drowning; crossing the road was always linked to being 'knocked down' and swallowing an orange pip could so easily lead to appendicitis, peritonitis and even death!

My wife does not know how to worry in a serious way. She simply knows it is a pointless and unproductive exercise – we'll hear soon enough if anything is wrong. Thankfully she has been very understanding with my annoying weakness and puts her own disposition down to good fortune.

I was clearly tiring of my pernicious condition when I wearily confided the details to friends we were staying with in Wisconsin. Their surprising reply contained the seemingly strange information that my worries were only thoughts, and they suggested I should remind myself of this when plagued by uninvited intrusions into my mind. The timing must have been perfect because I immediately sensed that a new day was dawning in my experience – but very gradually, I am sorry to say. I'd so much like things to be put on fast forward. If past experience were anything to go by there would probably be some deep practical applications ahead to entrench this newly revealed truth firmly in my everyday living.

Two months later while sitting back home in a Canterbury restaurant, I found I could not hold myself erect at the table nor move the left side of my body.

It became evident I had suffered a stroke and I was soon on a stretcher and being wheeled off to hospital with the ambulance siren blasting a way through traffic. Unable to move about under my own steam, I needed a month in a recovery ward, and occasional home visits meant being pushed around the village in a wheelchair. Used to seeing me out and about in running gear, the locals thought I had fallen over while on a training run. I soon discovered that I had so much to cope with physically that I had no spare time to worry about other people, not even my close family and their illnesses, which had always been the main targets for my worrying disposition. I could not let them live their own lives and take their own risks.

Strangely enough, this slightly more relaxed attitude quietly persisted and, once discharged, I found it relatively easy to dismiss worrying thoughts as perverse and uninvited guests. I didn't resist them – that didn't work – but just watched them pass me by.

I just concentrated hard on getting mobile again and began at last to appreciate what many invalided people suffer day in and day out. When I finally overtook my first human being – a frail old lady dragging a shopping trolley up a slight hill – it was to me the equivalent of an Olympic gold medal.

Intrusive thoughts did not give up easily. They had received a welcome for too long. But this was certainly another day. 'I am *not* a worrier,' I told myself, 'Just being plagued with unwanted worrying thoughts, that's all.' Please understand this was not merely a matter of semantics. I was not playing word games. This new attitude began to make a substantial difference to my enjoyment of living. It was not just the well-advertised 'power of positive thinking' with all the strain of striving to remember to think correctly and to say the right words. I was not whistling in the dark. I knew deep inside me that this new insight was absolutely true: these unwanted worrying thoughts did not originate in the deepest and holiest part of my being, they were not what I either wanted or believed.

Easily persisting with this truthful attitude, I continued to let any negative, destructive thoughts slip past me. Let me repeat, I did not resist unwanted worries or distressing feelings in my body, for I knew by bitter experience that what I resisted always persisted. A friend suggested I was more like a reed in the wind; if it resisted the force it would snap, because it bent, it survived.

If I failed, which I did quite often, then I accepted the pain this inevitably brought, and this quiet submission stopped the flow of a further adrenalin rush, so the anxieties gradually subsided. Lessons I had read about long ago in the valued writings of the author Doctor Claire Weekes (a GP who went on to specialise in nervous illnesses) began to pay dividends and I was slowly and persistently learning to undo the damaging thought-habits of a lifetime.

I soon realised how often severe adversity can change our perspective by giving us no alternative but to focus only on the present moment. I didn't promise never to worry again, but I felt quietly confident that I would be living on a different level and so it has proved.

The truth had once more set me free. The demon of worry has been exposed not as a constant winner, but as a fraud. Adversity, previously seen as grist for the mill of my constant worry, had been turned to my advantage as I have gone on to prove time and time again.

It is a great help knowing that tribulation is often the doorway to greater acceptance and a restful state of mind. Our hardships are not a test for us to pass or fail, set by a critical examiner. We can't cope and we don't try to, but leave it to a higher power within us, without concerning ourselves with our performance. It's good to leave it to Someone else!

Adversity has ever been considered the state in which a man most easily becomes acquainted with himself –

Dr Samuel Johnson

DON'T DO IT!

I suppose if we want to be pedantic, we could say that relaxing, flopping down inside and out, *is* doing something. But just as it takes fewer muscles to smile than it does to frown, we could decide to make no effort to hold ourselves respectably together. No effort – that describes it better.

Where I have shared these insights with fervently religious people they have often aroused great anger. Theirs is a do-it-yourself way of living, often kept alive by constant meetings, studies and exhortations to do better. The often-used picture comes to mind of someone continually going to the well for water rather than finding a river springing up within themselves. It is evident which one is the restful way of living. Try to follow the life-style of the Master and you'll find that crusade is a very hard taskmaster, equal in my mind to trying to run up the downward escalator when the alternative easy ride is only a few steps away.

That crazy illustration probably came to mind because as a young lad I tried running up the down side, as many do. Always been one for trying things and great fun it was too. That's all well and good as a fleeting novelty, but not good at all as a lifestyle; it just isn't the best way to reach the next level.

Once while doing a radio series in New Jersey I asked my host, 'Why won't people give up, just let go and live?' He shook his head as he replied, 'Most of us don't give up until we can't hang on any longer, Maurice.' I have found he was right; it is ingrained that we should try, try, try, instead of simply trusting the life inside us that lights up everyone that comes into the world.

A well-known speaker once commented to me that my wife was of a lovely disposition, but would get nowhere spiritually because she only lived in her safe area or comfort zone. When I chatted this over with Eileen she replied that she didn't want to get anywhere, she was happy where she was. I have found this to be true over sixty-four years of marriage and it is a mystery to me. There are other areas where she would like to be different, but not at the expense of leaving her own tranquil temperament.

It doesn't seem fair that it comes so easily does it? But then life is very far from fair as most of us have discovered, and many of us have accepted. A friend of mine says Eileen is an 'old soul' who has been here many times and has just about got her living where it should be. I have no inner response to that, no matter how much 'evidence' may be produced, but my mind is not closed. Eileen certainly has no ideas on the matter. She says life is as it is and we just might as well just live, being as helpful to each other as we can be without trying to change others to fit our mould. She is easy to live with.

There lies a really important lesson. Simply acknowledging the truth of the fact that life is as it is. This took me almost a lifetime to learn and I carried with me a resentment about the hand I had been dealt. I must have been only about eleven years or twelve years old when I went to the Saturday morning kids' 'pictures' and gazed on a beautiful Spanish woman singing, 'Que sera sera.' It was the first time I realised I was sexually aware, but it would have been more profitable if I had paid as much heed to the wise words as I did to her looks and her seductive voice. But hey, never mind, whatever will be will be.

When all else fails, do nothing!

JUST AN OLD WEEPIE

Sometimes it seems we'll never find a solution to some of our emotional or mental hang-ups. The Universal Providence seems either deaf or uninterested. Illumination totally eludes us as we ache to move ahead for the benefit of ourselves and others suffering with us. The ancient proverb, 'Hope deferred makes the heart sick,' invariably comes to my mind at such times as these.

As I have explained, my main distress concerned my inordinate concern for my family and the constant failure to let them live their own lives. 'You've never let them go!' my well-meaning colleagues would often point out. Easier said than done, I felt. But God knows I really wanted to get off their backs, for my overbearing concern for them has been a lifelong attitude, doing them no good at all. There is a world of difference between being available for someone and driving them crazy with attempts to prevent their suffering.

As always, I was looking for an instant cure-all, but soon learned from a hypnotist that it might take many months, many tears and many boxes of tissues – not to mention a great deal of money – to uncover the root of the problem. I decided to postpone the hypnotic approach to avoid stress after my recent stroke.

Informally chatting socially with a psychotherapist friend of mine, who was also a local vicar, we discussed – again – my persistent feeling of deep inner sadness even while being the life and soul of the party. I somehow knew this all sprang from way back in early childhood, with all those fears sown by my over-anxious mother and fearless father who just failed to understand. My late discovery, aged eighteen, of the adoption itself didn't seem to account for the underlying emotion of *sadness* and what it had to do with my possessiveness I could not see.

While we were still talking I somehow *knew* what the problem was that had dominated my early years and was causing such continual sadness now in adult life: I was lonely. This in spite of the company of a wonderful, patient wife who was always a silent listener to my ever-garrulous conversation. Yes, that was it; I was lonely.

Loneliness was subtly at the root of all this family fussing, I was sure. I had an inkling of this some years before, but had been told (perhaps a little harshly) by a prominent Christian Minister that I was just being self-centred and that I had far more friends than anyone else he knew. But then, it has often been said that you can be at your most lonely in a crowd.

At the time I was reading a splendid novel by Susan Howatch in which a man was experiencing severe problems relating to his adult children. 'Join the club!' I thought. This man was also found to be inflicting his own problems and his own misunderstanding of his children's situations onto his family. And so was I. If I was sad and lonely, then I assumed they must be too and needed my constant attention.

Sitting up in bed with the book laid aside, I found myself transported back in time to scenes I had completely forgotten, the times when I felt desperately lonely in my earliest years – the only child of older adoptive parents with no understanding of my young world. They just could not relate to me. There was virtually no contact between us, emotional or physical.

'You only eat and sleep here,' my mother would complain. What else was there to do? There were no siblings, no books to read and no games to play – the Meccano set came far too late, after my father's boss said his son had outgrown it. There was nothing to do but go out and rake the streets. No TV in those days. Mum seemed always ill and inactive and Dad worked terribly long hours in a factory, miles away from home. It was a very lonely life.

I felt the pain of loneliness surface from memories deep inside me, and wept.

As a child I was rather a weakling and quite a coward, so I got bullied on my long walk to school and back twice each day. Dad had been a boxer in his youth and, as I said, he was a fearless man. When I told him my fear of being beaten up all he could say was: 'The bigger they are the heavier they fall, son.' That didn't seem to work if you were running away. Nobody seemed to understand so, as I grew into my teens, I joined a street gang, probably to feel more secure in numbers.

Memory after memory came flooding back – I won't weary you with them all – and the tears kept flowing out. The therapist had been right about the tissues. As I cried I could see why I had clung to my grown children so much.

I had thought it was because they still needed me, but it was because I needed them, to stave off my loneliness. I had many friends who respected me and kept in touch faithfully, but I still always felt sad without pinpointing the problem. I was sad because I felt lonely.

No wonder I left my friends' greeting cards on display for so long. 'We love you, Maurice,' they read; 'You have been such a great help, Maurice,' and similar comments. I had to keep them there to remind myself that I was popular and I would go to any lengths to avoid offending anyone and risk the possibility of losing their friendship. The forthright Minister had been right, I was self-centred, but his harsh comment didn't help me.

I can now remember with a smile how my wife and I had a light-hearted arrangement that she would not die first, because I am completely inept in the home and can hardly boil an egg. I probably developed that calculated ineptitude to a fine art, for some women enjoy looking after a weak man. Many men hide behind their strengths, but I have always hidden behind my weaknesses.

But now I can imagine the true reason behind our jocular arrangement: I didn't want to be left alone. I was frightened of being lonely again. We can be so adept at protecting ourselves from pain that we usually don't know we are doing it, but now the light had been turned on. The truth was out and things would undoubtedly start to change.

I had always tried to help my family cross the road of life without walking in the puddles, but they have eyes of their own and have to learn to use them. Besides, walking in puddles can be fun! They are not my responsibility now. I am here if they need me, as I know they are available for me; but we are equals now. We are all adults. The loosened grip reduces my anxiety and helps their self-confidence. I am thankful we are all still friends in spite of my tiresome fussing.

As a family we have known more than our share of pain – as a lot of people have – but I become increasingly aware that in some mysterious way it is intermingling for our eventual good.

I am grateful for such a growing assurance and, even if it is assailed by doubt at times, nothing stops it being true: I am no longer desperately trying to cling to some kind of comfort, since Something (Someone?) comforting has taken hold of me, now.

At the innermost core of all loneliness is a deep and powerful yearning for union with one's lost self –

Brendan Francis

AN END TO SEPARATION

You will have by now realised that I usually rendezvous with reality at Wits' End Corner. Perhaps it's when all human strength has been expended and my raging soul is exhausted into listening stillness. I believe that is true for many of us. It is then that we seem to become utterly real and completely honest, holding nothing back, ready to hear our true inner voice whatever the content. It may not be that way for everyone, although I am convinced that, as the ancient parable says, seed that falls into honest ground does bear much fruit.

As I have already indicated, suffering can play a big part on our pathway of discovery, and I am just now reminded of a time when I was once more experiencing a deep sadness, sharing in the pain of my close family. In this emotional condition I turned on the six o'clock news and was assailed further by pictures of the intense suffering of maimed and dying children in the Balkans, of torn families wrenched apart by ethnic atrocities.

On top of my own personal sorrow it was the final straw. What a world! I climbed the stairs to my bedroom and cried myself out.

With what breath I had left I complained to the Power who had created all things and who seemed then to have deserted the handiwork, declining to intervene yet again. Coming from a then Christian perspective – although I am sure the same would hold for anyone coming from any other religious or humanistic perspective – I realised doctrine was not going to help me now. Once again I needed a life-giving touch, but I didn't harbour much hope.

'Don't you ever cry?' I croaked hoarsely. 'Don't you ever cry over the terrible anguish in the world *right now?* I thought you were supposed to understand about the desolation of the human soul!' My searing complaint was along those lines and I didn't expect an answer. I was just unloading.

That was when that rare, but unmistakeable stillness descended. I knew better than to move. Lying face down on my bed I could almost feel the physical weight of the silence and my histrionics were silenced. There was a depth to the stillness that would be impossible to exaggerate as I felt the import of the whispered words that gently rose up within me:

'I am lying on that bed crying now . . .'

That was all. But it was enough. My grief had caused me to forget what I thought I had learned through many years of experience – that the fundamental source of life, the essential Being that is the Universe (or God, if you find this name helps) and I were one. He was All and in all. I can only simply tell you that this encounter further changed my perspective, as it always does. I once again realised that the creator and the creation were wrapped up in the very same bundle of life. Not merely transcendent, sitting far above our suffering, but feeling it all in this moment. Not only living in us, but *as* us. I had already known this as a fact of information, but obviously a deeper experiential 'knowing' was needed to bring solace to a man sick with sorrow and exhaustion.

This certainly would not have been the plan we would have opted for, but it is painfully evident we do not see the whole or final picture. I once resided in Romford, a town in the county of Essex where Francis Quarles lived in the seventeenth century.

He exhorted his fellows not to 'judge the play before the final act' and I recalled these timely words when something of the eternal peace began to course gently through my veins once more.

Even without all the answers we can go forward knowing we go *as* the omnipresent power, ever in human weakness and dependence, but under-girded by a quiet confidence. The pain may persist, but it is cradled in a peace that passes all understanding. We are secure in the knowledge that it is all within us. It is not to do with feelings, but simply a quiet knowing. Some of us will make an obvious impact, some a behind-the-scenes contribution, but all of us hopefully not too aware of any good we may do. For we are just being ourselves.

If the Christ of Galilee should ever say to us (any of us, be we Christians or not), 'When I was in prison you visited me, when I was thirsty you gave me a drink,' hopefully we would reply as of old, 'When did we do this? When did we see you?'

But in deeper moments we understand a little more: for to embrace another living soul is to embrace the Eternal, the Divine. There is no separation; we are all of a piece. A touch of harmony is restored to our understanding. I believe much of our painful labour is to bring to birth this inner knowledge, so that even though we may so often feel a part of the problem, we also know we are also part of the answer.

I do not pretend that this knowledge will satisfy all our questions or remove all the mystery, but it can cause us to possess an underlying peace within our personal lives amid the global turmoil that is causing such unprecedented pressure and upheaval. It can put the mystical power of resurrection into bodies that sometimes feel they hardly have the strength to proceed another step.

I wouldn't want you to think that my entire life has been sorrow, doom and gloom! Far from it. I have enjoyed marvellous peaks of exhilarating joy. But it probably is true that my most formative spiritual experiences have been when any insights gained have been forged in the furnaces of some deep anguish or other.

There *can* be some joy in the midst of our sorrow, and a rainbow for us to trace through the rain, even though I confess at times of family distress I have almost despaired that the mist would ever clear. Perhaps I always will know times like this, for I seem to be a very late developer, one who is being carried along in spite of myself. As Muhammad Ali, that magnificent boxer, Muslim and philosopher said, 'If they can make penicillin out of mouldy bread, they can sure make something out of you.'

Sometimes I realise how our internal priceless treasure, that awesomely holy essence of eternity, is certainly buried in some very chipped and battered human treasure-chests!

A cracked pot lets the candle within shine forth

DRAW A BIG CIRCLE

We were aboard the morning flight to JFK. My wife had claimed her usual window seat and I waited to see who would complete our row of three.

Presently we were joined by a middle-aged lady dressed in a beautiful sari. She occupied the aisle seat next to me.

Our conversation flowed easily as we cruised at thirty thousand feet. I soon discovered she had flown from Mumbai (then Bombay) several hours before and was on the second leg of her journey to relatives in New York. Her home was on Marine Parade, known to me as 'The String of Pearls', so named because of the sweep of the lamps along the Bombay coastline. As I had served in the Indian Army many years before and knew her location, this made an immediate point of contact.

Showing little sign of fatigue, this gracious lady (being in the aisle seat) insisted upon getting us whatever we needed from the stewardess.

As we talked of India and England, and the differences in culture and religion, it was evident that, even if our understanding was different, we were of one spirit. There was no inner clash, no stridency, no insistence that our view was the only correct one.

My understanding of God at that time had come only through my encounter with Christ, hers through the many expressions of God that her Hindu upbringing had taught her. Thankfully we did not try to convert one another, but spent the hours listening to each other. We were engrossed, fascinated, enlarged and thoroughly grateful to have met. As we prepared to leave the aircraft our new friend touched my arm and I saw she had tears in her eyes. She said quietly, 'How do people cope in the world today, Maurice, without knowing God?'

The age difference, the miles, the cultures, the religions, had all been spanned because we wanted to learn from each other, because we all acknowledged there was a light that lights everyone that comes into the world and we sought that light in each other.

How fitting is the common Eastern greeting, 'Namaste!' – meaning 'I salute the divine within you.'

Our journey across the ocean had been a sheer delight instead of a head-on collision between two opponents and ideologies.

The warmth of that encounter lasted a very long time and returns whenever I recall the flight. I realise more than ever that I do not have to deny my own experience to grant that someone else's is also valid. I have no monopoly on the truth. Three non-judgemental souls had shared several happy hours, served each other and talked of intensely personal spiritual matters. That would have been impossible in my former hard-line days, when I belonged to an exclusive club and thought mine the only true story, my name for the Almighty the only acceptable name. I am sure that He (do pardon me, ladies) has no problem. My offspring call me the names of quirky TV personalities, like Victor Meldrew and Captain Mainwaring, but what does that matter if they love me? I am not worried because I know who I am, and I am quite sure our creator has no identity crisis.

Jesus Christ, the one who made all my house lights come on, taught me how to draw a big circle and be inclusive.

I believe he would have been horrified if I had failed to discern the true spirit of the Indian lady and had quibbled about correct words, which are surely but clumsy symbols of inner truth. Judging by outward appearances, the charming lady from Bombay and myself seemingly had nothing in common, but looking beyond the surface we found the truth, that we were one person and filled with one spirit.

You don't have to agree, to be united

A STUDY IN BLACK AND WHITE

You will remember that in an earlier chapter I related my experience on a grey, wet weekend in the Peak District. This lesson was hugely intensified during a 'dark night' of depression and frustration. It seems there are occasions in our life when we make great strides forward and we know we will never be quite the same again. At least, that appears so for those of a certain temperament.

Although we may make these seemingly sudden discoveries, usually the process has been lengthy. In this instance my capstone was lowered into place by a post-stroke neuropsychologist who pointed out that although I had taught many people to live in the grey areas of life, I still operated largely in black and white mode myself. That is the way I had tried to solve my own problems all through my life, but answers in life are not as simple and clear as I had so often made out.

Many others, Adolf Hitler and Margaret Thatcher to quote extremes, have done the same – though I do not imply they make happy bedfellows – and the long-term results have been devastating in quite different ways. So have many of my impetuous decisions, based as they have been upon an over-simplified and negative outlook. Now it seems was the time to consolidate earlier lessons of correct thinking.

Thankfully my consultant did not say I had to become a positive thinker, for I have always known that just becoming ultra-positive was not the answer to my negativity. Being exhorted to pull ourselves up by our bootlaces has caused too many breakdowns. There was a need quietly to appraise each situation in the light of reality, or the facts as best known to me at the time.

About a year after I suffered a stroke, a depression had settled on me that had reduced me to constant inactivity. The stroke was soon to be followed by immensely tragic family circumstances that it would be insensitive to unveil here. Being out of circulation and unavailable meant my correspondence dropped drastically when I failed to reply – that and the advent of email.

Visitors could not come because I soon became overtired. In addition to my incapacity and the tragedy, I now had to cope with seeming redundancy. Until now I had convinced myself I was living life as a human being not a human *doing!* However, it was now evident that, without someone for me to entertain, help, or give counsel to, I was far from being a satisfied personality.

Returning home from the neuropsychologist, I was determined to be less black and white and take a more rounded view of things, which seemed to be a daunting task. But it wasn't. It seems that much of the spadework had been done over the period of hard labour, experienced as depression and loneliness. Further assistance soon appeared in the form of an understanding lady in our neighbourhood who was both a friend and a qualified therapist. This counsel, along with the well-timed discovery of several books from the Mind, Body, Spirit counters of High Street bookshops, was of inestimable value. Again an ancient mystic saying proved true: 'When the pupil is ready the master appears.'

After months of serious complaining I knew I had slipped into yet another gear, another dimension of living.

One more step along the way. Someone once told me I was 'all crisis and no process', but that wasn't true now; there was plenty of process – maybe a lifetime of it? Life was proving far from just a series of black and white crises. One major contributory step was to make an un-pressured decision to be content in whatever circumstances came my way. Not to *make* myself content by putting on a perma-smile, pretending to be happy. Just a *decision to be so* and then to wait for any results to appear. It was just a different mindset, that is all, and before long a sense of quiet relief and contentment had settled upon me. If the miseries started to return I did not panic but quietly reiterated my intention to be content – yes, even content with the miseries! I suppose it was a kind of commitment to happiness, I don't really know; but I do know that the mind was stronger than my feelings. I really want to stress that this was easy to do, because I was not trying to accomplish anything, just taking up a new position, as it just seemed the right time to do so.

Looking back, I can now see I really wanted to be different, not only for my own sake, but for those closest to me. That desire had taken time to develop. I was not being asked, 'Do you want your situation changed? Do you want your life made easier?' But 'Can you accept life is as it is right now and just choose contentment?' Many people I talk to want other people to change, for instance, or their circumstances to improve, and then they feel they will be happy. Well, they may be for a short while, but then in difficult times their old attitude will start to reassert itself and they will need something else to satisfy them. Wanting things always to go our way is a never-ending treadmill and I had really wanted off.

As I write, several years after the initial experience, I can testify to the benefits even after many slip-ups. I hope my wife would back this up for she has been the forbearing subject of my niggling fussiness over detail for many years. I will give you a very small 'for instance' (the good salesman's essential words).

Granted it is a petty example, but then I have always appreciated the proverb, 'It is the little foxes that spoil the vines' – and perhaps 'take care of the pennies and the pounds will take care of themselves,' will do equally well to justify its inclusion:

> 'Would you like to go out for a drink this evening, dear?' I enquired.
>
> 'Yes,' Eileen called from upstairs, 'What shall I wear?'
>
> 'Why don't you wear what you have got on?' I shouted back.

Now that was a first! For over fifty years of married life I had been fussing about what Eileen wore or whether she had a strand of hair out of place. No wonder many of our friends think she deserves a sainthood for coping so ably with my perfectionist ways.

As I ponder the past years now, it seems as if I've been standing at a gateway for so long, holding it open encouraging others to go in and enjoy the pastures of happiness, but was unable to go in myself. I was too busy worrying about matters of very small import as you can see.

Now set aside by age and illness, with no-one to counsel, I was forced to seek earnestly my own contentment if I was not to end my days as a miserable old has-been, boring everyone with endless stories of my exploits in the heady days gone by.

Gradually, but increasingly, I began to feel genuinely content with my lot; I even ceased complaining that life was not fair, which is patently evident, as any sensible person already knows. Problems had not all suddenly disappeared, but I had now assumed a new perspective and I trust I shall continue to do so. Even as I write, a serious family illness has returned and my insides are starting their habitual wobble. It is time gently to assert my contentment with this moment, even if I do allow myself just a little hope for that special someone-else's future. I can no longer find a simple answer to everything as I once thought I should be able to do.

If you were to ask me now, 'What has been the most rewarding thing to happen to you in the past ten years?' I would surprisingly answer, with hindsight, 'A stroke that put me in hospital for a month, stopped me in my tracks and caused my ever-hectic lifestyle to dry up.' I had to be still.

Prospects for another London Marathon were clearly ruined as I was reduced to a long period of learning to walk again. There is no doubt I was extremely fortunate and in a year or so you could hardly discern a limp – well, not over short distances at least.

Undoubtedly one great spin-off has been my new independence from other people. The ability to stand alone was something I had often written and spoken about. But Eileen had been the wind beneath my wings for many years and I don't know how I would have survived without her support. Now I find I can increasingly fly alongside her, operating in what I believe therapists and psychologists call interdependence – or 'collaboration' to quote the learned author Scott Peck. A friend from Arizona once referred to Eileen as my PR lady. Perhaps she meant that others can observe how someone of her delightful disposition has stayed with such a vacillating perfectionist for over sixty years and then conclude I can't be all that bad!

At this point I am reminded of the time, twenty-three years ago – before most of the recent trials began – when we were preparing to move to our present small cottage in a Kentish village.

I felt my itinerant usefulness might be over and I was being put out to grass. Of course, I wanted to know what was the point of such a move. You can see how unbearably full of purpose I have been. Day and night, I bombarded the heavens with my grievance.

'You are going to have your mind renewed,' was my insistent internal answer.

Having always been more of a disaster on the emotional front, I felt this area should have received the priority but somehow, even back then, I vaguely understood that wrong thinking lay behind the painful emotional turmoil I so often experienced. Yet I did not know how to change. The emotive reactions to negative, black-and-white thinking had for many years flashed around my body, affecting various parts of my anatomy at the unstoppable speed of light. The link between fearful wrong thinking and my feelings has caused me a lifetime of emotional and physical havoc, not to mention distress to my family.

This stretch of life's journey has been a very long haul and a painful one, too. However, I am now thankfully reaping some rewards in this life, saving me from relegating all hope to the familiar 'pie in the sky when we die' theology.

Nevertheless, being a firm believer in the hereafter – and I do not press this upon you – I am convinced that the benefits will be carried over. But I will have to wait and see. Well that's not such a bad deal, is it, even if the many restless nights and miserable days at times tempted me to believe I was on an endless conveyor belt with no end product. What seemed so hopeless for so long has turned to modest hope since I began to feel that I have been in good hands all the time. I was greatly encouraged to press merrily on along the road of discovery.

Grey Is the Colour of Hope – Memoir by Irina Ratushinskaya

FLYING HIGH?

I wouldn't be surprised if by now you have a few big questions. How is this crazy old fellow doing today? Has he been continually flying smoothly at thirty thousand feet? The truth is 'No.' There have been quite a few storms and considerable turbulence. Where did we pick up the idea that the successful spiritual life is a repose in a rose garden? For those living in the real world and not a protected environment, there are often hard knocks along the way.

Much in the many religions on offer can lead us astray in this matter. My own experience has been largely Christian, where I was sold an ideal insurance policy. It said that if I could somehow find enough faith to believe the right things I would get a free ticket to a place called Heaven, with fully paid-up insurance protection and guaranteed comfort on earth until I reached the pearly gates. It took me far too long to discover the flaws in this doctrine.

Snatching a few bible texts here and there can easily back up this kind of teaching.

Snatching a few texts from elsewhere can give a very different picture – the Bible can be invoked to prove anything at all, it be made out to say anything we want it to say. But, hopefully, we will forever forsake that road – if we were ever foolish enough to embark upon it. I had years of such an approach with the ever-attendant dark angel of deep, crippling guilt cruising around me, ready to land on my head whenever I failed to live a blameless and thoroughly victorious life. There was always something I had done wrong, not done enough of, or done too much of. Too little faith, too little prayer; too much doubt, too much worry. If things went well God got the credit, if things went badly I got the blame. It was a no-win situation.

The 'name it and claim it' good news proclaimed by the Health, Wealth and Happiness Brigade is in fact very bad news. It is not the whole truth by any means. Such an approach may be a good framework for triumphant high-powered meetings but it can lead to endless heartache in real life when you can't drum up enough of the faith you are supposed to have to claim your promised inheritance successfully.

'[Jesus] always causes us to triumph!' is a text attributed to the apostle Paul. Challenging words, aren't they? It is well to recall that Paul, this great hero, once escaped from Damascus during the night hidden away in a basket.

Perhaps he did gently lift the lid and continue to whisper, 'He always causes us to triumph,' I don't know. However, I am sure he did not expect the sort of easy ride I hear propounded today to folks suffering with cancer, deep depression, horrendous family distress or financial disaster.

One fervent lady told me I had not brought up my children in the 'fear and admonition of God' – another text from the bible – and that was why my family was suffering so much serious illness. Several told me I should have more faith. Well thanks very much. I was a very polite Holy Joe in those days; today I think I might (as graciously as possible) invite these Job's comforters to take a long walk on a short pier! Years later while I was standing in the dole line for benefit payment I had to listen to the first lady complaining that her husband had served as a shop manager for many years and had now been made redundant.

It was so unfair, she indignantly proclaimed. Since when has life been fair? Ask any abused or starving child. Why do we 'believers' think we are entitled to special treatment? If there is a magic cure for all ills, why is it so difficult to find?

I do not write as one who has not seen miracles. I have – but just a few. A lifetime of experience has taught me that we cannot get God to pull all the right strings and order the world to our liking. The Almighty will not jump through our hoops. Once we can live comfortably with paradox and enigma, the 'Not Fair' syndrome has lost its grip on our lives. There are storms in life. Severe storms. Some of them may last a lifetime. Some things we shall never fully understand, but if we are weak enough to live in dependence upon the Higher Power we shall find we are strong enough to survive and live contentedly, just one day at a time. We shall keep the tell-tale twinkle in our eyes, albeit very faintly at times, as we once again trace the familiar rainbow through the rain.

Another well-meaning friend told me that we are not meant merely to survive, but to triumph gloriously. Very often, walking in the shoes that some people have to wear continually *is* to triumph gloriously. Even so it is good to arrive at a place where we can increasingly say, 'I know how to be up, I know how to be down, to be appreciated or humiliated; I have learned whatever state I am in, to be content.' That is something that has to be discovered in the school of life. We eventually learn that our reactions – our silly, wrong thinking – is what causes our suffering and thankfully for me this has largely dried up.

I am currently kind of walking (rather slowly at my age) gently alongside myself, observing what is happening, as I unlearn so many of the foolish rules and customs I have been taught since I came into the world.

Well, does that satisfy everyone's questions about my current performance? I shouldn't think so for a moment. But let me assure you that all my questions haven't been answered either. But they really don't matter at all since I stopped measuring my progress. I mean ever.

Except when I forget! Then I find myself smiling a little and going back to living in the awareness of this moment. Life is just as it is. My altimeter is out of action. I may be skipping on hills that are alive with the sound of music, or languishing for a while in dungeon despair (to accommodate Julie Andrews and John Bunyan in the same sentence); but as I said, it doesn't matter – nothing does when I am seeing aright. I have stopped digging up the recently planted seeds to see how they are getting on and to check that they are growing properly! All is well, since I have abdicated my responsibility to succeed.

Over recent years I have slipped almost effortlessly into the enjoyment of a tangible silence and stillness. There is a sense of spaciousness around and within me. It is very difficult to describe this awareness of my inner life, my true Being, which has overcome a hitherto unruly mind. The mind noise – that constant background static – is under control. There is peace in the Presence of The Other. Oh, how we struggle to express the unexplainable with our limited words but I guess if the time is right something will register and the dawn will begin to break.

To quote my friend, the inspirational songwriter, Dave Bryant, it has been a 'smooth and rocky road.'

A diamond is a lump of soot made good under pressure

THE AMAZING BLUE MINI

It is forty-five years since I gave up my position as a sales manager to begin life as an itinerant speaker with no stipend. The family were going to live by any gifts folk cared to give me as a reward for any blessing I might have brought them. It was called 'living by faith'. I well remember a very cold day when I had deferred turning the heating on to save money. Another minister called in on us and remarked, 'Man, you are not living by faith you are dying by faith.' It was not very encouraging but probably true.

Soon after this our youngest son, aged five years, asked me, 'Dad, why don't we have a car like we used to?' I did my best to explain why we couldn't afford to buy one and that I travelled by public transport now. 'Why don't you ask God for one?' he asked. I told him I did not have any faith so there was no point. It was bedtime as we climbed the stairs along with his brother, who was one year older.

Once by the bed I said, 'Matthew, do you think God will give me a car?' 'Yes,' he said most sincerely. So I asked *him* to pray. He willingly knelt by the bed with his brother Jason and said, 'Dear God, please send Daddy a Blue Mini,' and then the boys popped into their beds. I must admit to thinking, 'A pity he didn't ask for a Jaguar,' but it didn't really matter because I was sure there was no chance of a favourable response to such a childish prayer.

The next day, a Saturday I remember, I left home in Canterbury and caught the train to London Victoria before transferring stations *en route* for Reading. There I found a small front room crammed with young people ready to listen to my stories – what one person had previously called my 'Dripping On' and which led to a magazine series under that heading. So I dripped on in Reading for over an hour (no ten minute sermons in our movement) and a gentle stillness crept over the room. It was quite some minutes before a young man asked, 'How did you get here, Maurice?' 'By train,' I replied.

He then asked if I had a car and I informed him, 'Not at the moment.' At which point he threw his car keys across the room saying, 'Here, have mine. It's the blue Mini outside.' To say I was surprised would be an understatement; I was gobsmacked!

When I phoned home the next morning I told Eileen I would be coming by car, but didn't mention what type of car it was. The boys were peering out of the upstairs window as I drove round the roundabout next to our house. 'It's a blue Mini, it's Dad!' they cried as I drove up, so Eileen told me. There had been no doubt the request would be answered.

And that is evidently the secret. No doubt in your heart. My son had not been childish, but child*like*; there is a world of difference. In our sophistication that godly attribute has largely been lost. But I won't try and explain the situation. It will have to remain part of the great Mystery that I constantly eulogise about. Oh, I have plenty of ideas, and scriptural verses I could put forth, but I have thankfully ceased looking for answers for everything. However, I do know that the man who turned the radiators off has not wanted for family needs for forty years, although we have been down to our last few slices of bread before now.

At other times we have abounded financially and have certainly become simpler people who may at times be knocked down, but are never knocked out. Many will have their own explanation for the 'Case of the blue Mini' and that's OK. I have no doubt where the gift came from and I'm sure you can guess what I believe. Life is much easier since I learned to live with enigma, paradox, and without answers to all my questions. It's a pity I never got that Jaguar . . . but better still, I could fill a small book with similar stories.

Take therefore no thought for the morrow:

for the morrow shall take thought for the things of itself.

Sufficient unto the day is the evil thereof - King James Bible

COMING BACK HOME

I am now embarking on my tenth decade, and quite a number of years have passed since I finished the first draft of this manuscript. I had just passed the seventy-five year milestone. In the book I was currently reading, I came across the story of a seventy-five year old man who had carried a passion for reality since he was very young. Just like me. Maybe because of the synchronicity of the ages I was especially interested.

It seems that this young, eager fellow set out in search of truth and travelled all his life across many lands and many seas. There was rugged terrain with high mountains and deep ravines to cross, so he experienced a great deal of hardship and suffering. One day, with three-quarters of a century in years behind him, he realised he had not found what he was looking for and returned home. When he finally arrived back home it was to discover that truth, or reality, had been patiently waiting there for him through all those years. I feel sure you will have heard the same story in one form or another.

Did the man's journeying enable him to find the truth he sought? I am sure the answer is *'No, not really; but it helped him to recognise it!'*

Although it may not seem like it, we actually only discover what has been there all the time. If you protest that surely we must grow and not just remain young and immature, I can only respond by saying that our progress or journey is really a growth in awareness of what has always been within us – but hidden in unawareness all through the years.

It is when we finally cease to struggle and come back home to rest that we can enjoy the acceptable reality of the moment. Things are right, just as they are, in spite of all other appearances. They are in a way strangely 'easy' even if our circumstances are painful and we are pushed to the limit. We already have within us all that is necessary for life and godliness. They were here with us, within us, all the time. But we couldn't see it. Our light had become darkness, that is all. Now the light has emerged and we can see again. And we don't all have to struggle on until we are seventy-five to realise this.

Many of us know the mythical story of mankind eating from the tree of the knowledge of good and evil, thereby losing the ability to eat from the tree of life. That is another way of expressing what we are considering here. Thankfully, I have fallen out of the branches of the first tree and no longer judge what is good and bad anymore. Some of the things that seemed extremely evil to me at one time I can now see have given me the most lasting benefits.

Even as I write that old stroke health-scare has reared its head again, but that is how it is. I don't need to categorise and label the experience so that I can start to worry about it. I am not saying I like the symptoms or that they are pleasant, just that, *in this moment,* I am full of acceptance towards the matter. Then I will take whatever action is necessary. It is a great day when we cease to wrestle with every seeming misfortune that comes our way.

Maybe it would be helpful just to breathe deeply repeatedly right now. I am very seriously suggesting that right now could be a good time to be still and consciously accept this moment for what it is and what it has brought.

This may be the time for some of the mists to clear away and for the wonder of our inner life to emerge into the foreground. Circumstances are secondary now. The Presence is our comfort as spaciousness, and the consciousness of our union with all things, becomes the primary factor in our lives.

Is my marathon journey finished then? Or have I a few more miles to go? Who knows? Better still, who cares? I have finally returned home and am enjoying being still, having ceased to keep picking at the irritations of life and turning them into festering crises. But if I should be tempted to walk a few miles off the main path and have another look at that seductive tree of good and evil, hopefully I will soon realise my foolishness and return home to rest again.

I seem to be using a lot of mixed metaphors, but – as our friends across the pond say – I hope you catch my drift!

I have just remembered one of those precious, relevant moments in life that happened round about my seventy-five year mark. I was visiting a friend in our village. It was a hot summer day and we were sitting on his lawn sipping some delicious, cold white wine.

The setting was very good! After listening to several of my stories Barry held my gaze and said earnestly, 'You've been seeking all your life, Maurice.' I knew he was right. I'd been a seeker and a finder and a seeker still. Always seeking. But as he spoke I somehow strangely knew that now my search was ended; just like the old man in the story I had come home.

Yes, the searching is over but the discoveries will surely continue. They will continue with stillness and contentment in my heart without all the previous strain and stress. The intensity has finished. As Barry and I sat together I could almost feel the presence of Alan, another elderly friend, creep up and whisper one of his favourite sayings in my ear, *'Stay detached, Maurice!'* He loves a glass of good wine, so I am not surprised he turned up in my imagination, and his wise observation indicates he too has learned a thing or two along the way.

It is several decades since I heard Bakt Singh and his story of Mount Everest, which I related in one of the first chapters of this little book.

As you can see, it has taken a very long time for me to learn how to be still and to wait for the mists to clear. Firstly, I *believed* in the majesty of the eternal silence and stillness, the presence that is always here but so frequently is not discerned or appreciated. The promise rang true, so I started to listen. After time I came to *know and occasionally experience* that presence for myself. Now at last I am *constantly aware* of it being at home within me, even when unruly feelings, unpleasant circumstances, or intruding voices are telling me otherwise.

It is has been a long, painful journey but so very worthwhile. And it continues.

There's no place like home

A STING IN THE TAIL?

Having just about reached the end of what I wanted to communicate there was a feeling that something was missing. After pondering for a while I realised I had avoided relating my very first experience of an other-worldly or consciously spiritual experience. Probably for fear that I might be labelled 'heavily religious' when organised religion, as opposed to spirituality, is something that I feel has probably been responsible for more harm than good. However, I am going to come clean, hoping that you will press through anything unpalatable and forego any judgement until the very end.

Well then, what *was* my first conscious experience of what I call God, but that I don't insist others do? You'll need to bear with me if you feel there is no Higher Power - or if you have heard a similar story before – this may well turn out to be very different at the end.

I had no such conviction about another dimension for nearly thirty years, but gazing up at the starry sky in my late teens I inexplicably felt a deep desire to know the truth of this matter, which led me to earnestly seek, both at home and abroad, to know if there was any meaning to my existence on this planet. Perhaps it was the feeling of a lack of wholeness, or what some have called a 'god-shaped hole' inside me. This all came to a head on May the fifth in 1955. I remember it as 5.5.55.

Shortly before this date I was seated in the back room of The Plough public house in Kingham in Oxfordshire, the village where our family was residing at the time. It was a well-lubricated meeting of the All Blacks Football Club of which I was the secretary. At the close the club chairman asked if I would visit the local Rector to see if he would become a Vice President of the club and make the usual financial contribution for the honour of being selected.

No-one else wanted to go for fear their request might be reciprocated with an enquiry as to their lack of church attendance. I readily agreed and a few days later, on May the fifth, made an evening visit to the imposing Kingham rectory.

After the rector had willingly parted with ten shillings and sixpence – half a guinea in the informal parlance of those days – I left the lounge and started to descend the long flight of stone steps into the courtyard to go home. It was a very dark night, I remember.

Suddenly I heard a clear voice call out, 'Is everything all right with your soul, Maurice?' I stopped dead in my tracks, turned round and opened my mouth with the full intention of saying 'Yes, thank you,' and hurrying away. Strangely, I found myself emphatically saying, 'NO!' I was bemused and was soon being led back into the rector's study. He obviously meant business. I was subjected to a familiar old story that others had related during my long search. It was about Christ dying for me, accompanied by an invitation to kneel and invite him to enter into my life and take control.

'No thank you!' I blurted, 'I don't really believe the story so there is no point.'

With that I made a hasty retreat feeling that the chaps in the pub were certainly right, this visit had led to trouble. Arriving home I headed straight for the bedroom, flung myself down on my knees and started addressing the upper stratosphere.

'I'm tired of this search. I don't know whether you exist or you don't. But if you do, then I give you full permission to reveal yourself to me.' Generous of me, wasn't it? With that I undressed and got into bed. I had promised nothing and expected nothing. All I had done was to be honest and open.

When I awoke after a full night of sleep I was in a different world. I felt a new man. My usual irritation with the futility of life did not assail me. Then I realised that the niggling pain from my duodenal ulcer was absent and I didn't crave my usual morning cigarette. I never smoked for forty years after that and an X-Ray showed the ulcer had disappeared.

Needless to say, I was delighted and told many people that I met about the experience. Not everyone was glad to hear my good news. However, I was sure the rector would be pleased so I hot-footed my way to find him to tell him I knew God and I had a new-found affection for his Son. That was all I knew.

But it wasn't to prove enough, as I soon discovered. I found the good man at the village hall where a dance was being held, probably for charity.

I tried to explain what had happened but he gave me no chance. 'You've become a Christian,' he said, 'I can see it in your face, you're radiant.' All I knew was I felt different and in some strange way inwardly knew there was a higher power, omnipotence, omnipresence or whatever, and I was in touch with the same. The rector obviously wanted to formalise this experience, to put it into a framework so that it could become the exclusive truth, although I didn't fully realise all this at the time. My unique experience had been given a name. I had been put into a special category. I was labelled.

It got worse. Inside the hall I encountered the rector's wife whom I had always admired for her warmth and cheerfulness. She, too, recognised the 'new man' in front of her and so two happy extroverts waved our arms about in celebration as the recorded music played in the background. 'Would you like to dance?' I invited, with exuberance.

Then came the next bombshell . . . 'Christians don't dance, Maurice.' I felt shocked, for I loved dancing. It was the first of a long list of things I mustn't do, or must do, in order to continue on my joyful path.

Other churched folk told me I shouldn't drink alcohol, I should pray early in the morning, I should be baptised and confirmed, should buy a bible, and remember: 'Billy Graham reads five Psalms and three Proverbs every day . . . and should you do less?' Well the joy didn't continue once I got entangled in this systematised religion. But I pretended it did and substituted a so-called 'deeper way' until years later, exhausted by formalised systems of religion, I returned to my first love where performance and what I did or did not believe, had nothing to do with my peace. Rules were abandoned and sheer grace took their place.

Over the years I have heard hundreds of similar stories – I call them 'variations on an original theme' – where a beautiful encounter with Truth, Love, Peace, call it what you will, has been spoiled, marred, and made ugly by formalising that which is beyond understanding, too wonderfully varied and immense to be totally encapsulated within any one belief, one pattern of practice and discipline, one holy book, one type of building, or one special experience.

Truth has been encountered in a myriad of ways and places and is recognised in the spirit of those who are still open to find it beyond their own experience. Oh how thankful I am that I can go outside and gaze up into the heavens, realising there are millions or billions of stars, suns, galaxies and universes, and I am just a speck. Not a mere speck, but a glorious speck, a part of an unspeakably majestic, infinite Mystery that is thankfully all too much for me.

The terrible cruelty of the natural world is all contained within such indescribable beauty; the pain and suffering in so many lands, man's inhumanity to man, is rubbing shoulders with touching kindness. Overtly humble I may not be, but stunningly, internally humbled I most certainly am. My answers are not all neatly in; there is always more unlabelled experience to be a part of. That is my meagre opinion to which you have been subjected.

Just small glimpses of truth are often all we get. Nobody can grasp, see, hold, disseminate or live in much of it at a time; it is too inordinately vast for all that.

It is spatially and spiritually infinite. Truth expresses itself in little lamp flashes between the trees, elusively blinking in the darkness, now here, now there, like a meadow full of fireflies. Chasing it, and hunting it down to possess it is a fruitless mission, like nailing down the end of a rainbow! Creator and created are so gloriously tangled up together that they are one breath, breathed together. Jesus said 'I am the truth,' and as I expressed earlier there is a sense in which we are too. Yet none of us is, or has, all of the Truth. Like spotting a shooting star, each incandescent burst of truth is an exhilarating excitement, but it will not be tied down, made captive or enshrined.

That most religions contain glimpses of truth I do not deny, and I can often and comfortably join in with them and be strangely moved at times. But please don't box me in; don't give me a name that describes my experience. It's all too big for that. I am overwhelmed, that's all. I am also overwhelmed by sadness at times and overwhelmed by irritation at times, but how good it is to be overwhelmed by acceptance, by being intimate with the Power through which everything consists, even if it is still engulfed in so much mystery.

It causes me to be still with wonder more and more and more. Even today I heard of someone who found spiritual solace in the quietness of a mosque. Now I suppose she is labelled a Muslim, just as I was labelled a Christian. Can't we see the unity of all people and all things, a glorious experience that does not need explaining? Maybe one day we will, or is that too much to hope for?

I am going to close this story by telling you of a journey I made with a young man many years ago.

He had just received a degree from Bristol University and was *en route* to Germany to take up a teaching post. He had successfully thumbed a lift and was subjected to my enthusiasm soon after my initial liberating experience. I told him how I had addressed the Unknown with an invitation to let me know the truth and opened myself to whatever: 'Do you exist? If so then please reveal yourself to me.' I said there could be no harm in him or anyone doing that, surely? His reaction stunned and amused me as he replied, 'Oh no, I would not do that . . . . *supposing it is tru*e!'

Once you label me you negate me –

Danish philosopher Soren Kierkegaard

LESSONS LEARNED ON E BAY

I keep ending this manuscript and then continuing. That is because this is a book of experience and life is ongoing, producing more and more stories.

In May 2012 I had another stroke after another urinary infection and completely lost my balance. Once more admitted to hospital I was greeted by another patient on the ward saying, 'You are the only patient I have ever seen come in here smiling.' Further ushered into a small section of four beds I noticed a large notice on the wall stating 'E BAY.' I half- wondered if I was up for sale on the internet, but only for a moment. One can become a little confused and disoriented in these places.

As I settled in, a tall rather academic kind of fellow called out from his bed, 'Hello Maurice!' I turned to find the Chaplain from the mental hospital where I had been a patient four years previously after a bladder infection. He also remembered me from some meetings I had taken part in many years ago at the Royal Albert Hall and other large London venues.

We found we had a few mutual acquaintances. This man became a real friend and helped me considerably with his spiritual understanding.

Peter was so interesting. A mountaineer, a musician and singer who knew his classical music and also his fifties, sixties and seventies pop music. These were the very years which I had missed through my heavily religious emphasis that ruled out nearly everything enjoyable except breathing. We played all this music on the radio in the evening with the lights turned down like a nightclub. We even had one of the female care assistants dancing for us in the bay, much to our enjoyment.

But Peter couldn't cope with my incessant talking – a real weakness I am afraid – so he sometimes used to close his eyes and nod off. I told him people had always encouraged me to speak and tell my stories, sometimes for hours on end, and now I was tired of it all myself but could not stop. It was commonly called 'dripping on' and some visitors would come to our house to be, as one of them put it, hosed down by my words. Now I was tired of my own voice.

Peter said, 'Well you can always shut your eyes, can't you?' Having previously seen him do this with me I caught his drift immediately.

Folk would always understand at my late stage of life if I gently closed my eyes. We smiled together when I commented that we had just composed a new proverb, '*He who shuts eyes also shuts mouth!*'

A few minutes after meeting Peter, a young neighbour of mine appeared in the bay doorway pushing a trolley with newspapers and magazines. We were both astounded and had a quick excited hug, for Teresa had started work in the hospital that very morning. I began to feel someone was on my side, but then decided this was just some form of synchronicity, the sort of thing that happens when you happily go with the flow. It is then that one notices these wonderful happenings, without getting overly spiritual and trying to define them all the time. Observing and accepting is so much better than the trying to understand-and-manipulate way; then the magic and the joy of living is lost.

Oh there are so many stories, none better than that of Akuti, the attractive young Nepalese nurse who brightened the ward on the days she attended us. The staff changed duties every day, probably so they wouldn't get involved with the aged patients who tried to engage them in constant banter. It was all rather silly.

I particularly wanted to talk to her sometime, as I had served alongside the world-famous Nepalese Ghurkhas on the North West Frontier between India (now Pakistan) and Afghanistan. So I speak a little Urdu and have patrolled many of the small towns and villages we hear about in the news during these troubled times.

I had been longing for a shower as I hadn't bathed properly since my admission to hospital. Akuti was leading back a spotlessly clean Malcolm, a seventy-nine year old fellow who had difficulty shuffling along. I had given up trying and smilingly said without intent, 'I expect my turn will come.' 'I'll take you now,' she replied, and off we strolled with her holding me upright. Once there she helped me undress and began soaping me from head to toe. Once she discovered my minimal, halting Urdu was similar to the Hindi she spoke, she was delighted and kept provoking me until more and more words came back after over sixty years. It was an enjoyable episode and full of laughter.

I didn't see my new friend for a few days, but she did come on the day of my discharge.

We again laughed for the final time and she mischievously said, 'We met too late, Maurice, but in the next life – who knows?' My wife and I now smile about the contact and she seems pleased I enjoyed myself with the coquettish young Akuti. As I type my beloved Eileen has just asked me what I'd like to drink, and she is looking absolutely splendid for her eighty-four years. I am sure I married the right lady – and little Akuti has probably bathed dozens of other old men and quite a few young hunks too, but she certainly helped cheer my stay as she stringed me along.

So this hospital stay had its moments. I have a notebook containing several amusing stories and a few upsetting ones, too, when an impatient ward doctor, a bullying male ward manager and a few insensitive care-workers temporarily impaired my dignity. Even though it was distressing it is also maybe understandable, as nearly everyone wants their attention this minute, when they are so overworked and understaffed. Overall it was an excellent ten days stay and one where I somehow learned in real life how to ask for nothing and watch everything come to me, enriching my life.

Perhaps one last poignant story will illustrate the words I have just written: With their diminished abilities some of the other stroke patients were always losing things, causing the staff to search every piece of clothing, the lockers and under the beds. Sometimes the staff became irritated and it didn't help much when I inadvisably pointed out that they had recently mislaid a patient. They were not amused, but I thought their frantic search very funny.

But then came my turn! During one of Eileen's visits I could not find my specs although she looked for them too. After she had gone I remembered a phrase I had heard, '*Relax and let things come to you.*' I laid back on the bed, untroubled by the loss. Some time later Malcolm called across that there were some glasses on his side table. I guided my Zimmer over to have a look and tried them on. They were certainly not made to my prescription. I looked at Malcolm's specs which were on his face and said, 'They look like mine, where did you get them?' 'Oh I picked them up somewhere' he blandly replied as we made a formal exchange.

I returned to my bed space and pondered what had happened. My spectacles had definitely come to me. I realised how enjoyable it was to relax more and gave up asking the nurses for help with everything I felt I needed. The timing was obviously right. It worked a treat as I peacefully received the odd cup of tea, an invitation to watch a cricket match through a huge picture window providing a close view right down the wicket on the Kent County cricket ground and several other unsought privileges. I felt I was being treated like a prince.

I know I am quietly going to enjoy consciously letting things come to me – 'In Your way and in your time', as the singer/songwriter Graham Kendrick wrote many years ago. It was always a favourite song of mine and now it was becoming a way of living. I found that letting time pass, not trying to kick any doors down, was a much more peaceful way of living.

Do be quite sure that I am not advocating sloppiness and irresponsibility, but just being easily and almost constantly aware of the present moment; living in the here-and-now, accepting life as it comes in the small situations such as I have mentioned – and in the major issues of life that can so easily cause us to panic and thrash around for answers. I have been living in this more conscious way for several years, but recently it seems to have much more firmly fixed in my psyche as the norm, and a condition that comes naturally and without strain. And that fixation came to me in its own good time.

Well, I am home again as I write and now off for a hot shower. I wonder if Eileen will soap me down? I am sure she won't, but she *will* lovingly watch to see I don't fall, because you can't really use a walking stick in the shower.

Relax - Let everything come to you

IN THE EYE OF THE STORM

Recently, as I crept upstairs for the night and laid my head on the pillow the above title popped into my head. Having thought that I'd already put this little book to bed, I mused, 'That would be a better way to end my little book.' So here I am writing to my moment of inspiration. I can do nothing without that; perspiration on the other hand does nothing for me, unlike some fine writers and songwriters I know.

For many years I had a secret longing that I would find a place where there would be continual blue skies. I just had to do the right thing to find it. My heavy, religious days had instilled this into me I feel sure. Still with my head on the pillow, the words from an old hymn ran through my head:

> The storm may roar without me,
> My heart may low be laid,
> But God is round about me,
> And can I be dismayed?

That's it, I thought with a wry smile. There is something round about me that is more dependable than my feelings. It is too big to describe. And it is not only round about me, it is in me, it *is* me. It is a deep internal Stillness that has been realised through the fires of a lifetime, as has been unfolded in some of the stories I have relayed.

Tomorrow I go for the results of some vital blood tests, having been called urgently back after other tests last week. The doctor is very concerned. But 'Can I be dismayed?' I suppose the total truth is, 'Yes, just a little, but not for long,' as I lean back once more into the truth of who I really am in the deepest part of my being. I am the observer again, watching the play of life's events and all is well. Will I be as calm tomorrow? Tomorrow never comes, life is always *Now*. Am I whistling in the dark? No. I know deep down inside that whatever I hear will be what it will be. Will I agree to aggressive treatment? I don't know, I don't have to answer that today, the question may never arise. Or it may; I was on a fast-track cancer investigation for some months last year.

Even as I write I have taken some involuntary deep breaths and a quiet smile has again crept across my face. I am grateful that the Stillness, God, the Unfathomable, All in all, Father, Mother – call the Presence what you will – is always here, waiting for our quiet focus, our consciousness, our awareness, our relaxation into the incredible No-Thing within and around us.

Thank you for reading my stories. As I close them down I am going to prepare for a short coach outing with the old folks from our village. They were 'poor old people' for whom I always felt pity when they passed me by in younger days. I am one of them now, needing to be helped up into the coach. It is all part of a wonderful, painful, ecstatic, bewildering and now peaceful journey that is nothing like I thought it would be or should be.

But what *do* I know? Very, very little in this immense, indescribable universe among universes, and yet it is enough.

I do know it is time for this speck, this glorious speck,
To wish you well and say goodbye

•

POSTSCRIPT: by Bridget Boyle

'LET EVERYTHING COME TO YOU' – A GUIDE TO HOW IT'S DONE

There isn't one! Some of you may have got to the end of Maurice's little book and have a fleeting twinge of secret disappointment. Perhaps you loved the title, for this is what you have long desired; maybe you have sought this magical Stillness in every creed and cult, every precept and practice, and hoped that this at last was 'IT'! Maybe you hoped that this would finally bring what you have yearned for with such aching hunger, feeling that as a hunted deer gasps for the water brooks, so your soul longs and thirsts for a living experience of God.

How often have I, too, felt that same anguish, only to return from that prayer still feeling parched of spiritual refreshment and arid of soul.

So I absolutely understand why you, like almost everyone else in the world (most certainly including me!) may be looking for a 'how to' book, ever seeking that one magic wand that makes everything all right, that perfect formula, the cure-all poultice, the ultimate alchemic liturgy that really does conjure up God's presence, that brings the genie out of the lamp, and that really does solve all the soul's dis-ease–

If only!! It’s so very hard to grasp the truth that it is so much easier than all that. Only those like Maurice who've been through it all, endured all those spiritual wild goose chases and have had the childlike courage to admit that the Emperor has no clothes, ***that it just doesn't work like that*** – only they can see beyond the yearning for 'how to' or for 'a guide to' and let all of that go. It can take a little while (if not a lifetime) to see and understand where Maurice is coming from ... but often it’s only when you’ve tried it all that you gradually understand something of the difference that is Maurice. *He* doesn’t know ‘How to’ either! But he does know that when you hunger and thirst, you shall be filled. You don’t have to know ‘How to’ fill yourself, you simply are filled.

Even some publishers want Maurice to analyse his insights and to explain 'How to' possess and live in the truth of them. But that's not how it works; Maurice can share his insights and through them encourage and inspire, but he cannot analyse and prescribe.

If an inspirational musician who produces and plays magically soul-moving cadences and harmonies is never invited to perform at the Barbican because he can't read music, playing only by ear and instinct from the core of his being, then many with a true musical heart stand to lose out. The adventure, the joy of musical discovery is not limited to those who learn the conventions and can read the musical script. If we seek to learn only from those who can tell us 'How to', then we will learn only a technique, a procedure, a dead shell, a fixed moulded cast. The Essence of Life will not be poured into a cast and moulded. This Essence is intangible, unconfined, amorphous and free as the wind; it is undefined and indefinable. If you try to encapsulate running water it isn't running any more.

There is no formula. But don't be disappointed!

Be we consciously filled full or perhaps feeling dry and unfilled, we are each one perfectly all right just the way we are right now. All is as it is meant to be. Somehow the universe and all things in it work together to the blessing and advantage of all those who have ever felt that deep-seated, homesick longing, a mystical, primordial yearning for the place they know they belong. It is happening. We shall be made still. We shall be filled full.

"All shall be well and all shall be well and all manner of thing shall be well."
(Julian of Norwich)

A POEM BY A FRIEND

by Phil Streeter

Don't hold me responsible for beliefs
That have probably changed by the time you
read these lines.
And above all,
Don't hold them up against me, demanding that I
live by them, and
prove them.
I don't want to prove anything!
Merely to stand in dumb desire and rollicking awe;
Open-mouthed with wonder and delight
At life's flickering moments of
Instant understanding,
surprise revelation and
flashes of simple beauty.

Don't you see that deepest beliefs are always the
most elusive,
Like strange exotic fish found in the darkest depths.

Like crystal waiting to catch the sun,
And like butterflies,
When you try to pin them down, you kill them.

About the author

Born in London in 1927, Maurice Smith had an unhappy childhood, feeling a misfit in his family. Not until he joined the army did he discover his true origins. The recruiting officer demanded to see a full Birth Certificate and, when the document arrived, it was headed Certificate of Adoption. For the first time, he discovered why he felt disconnected – and that his original surname was Fullard.

Faith and religion formed no part in his upbringing, but he began a conscious pursuit of a Higher Power one evening when he stared up at a starlit sky and was gripped with wonder. From that moment, he sought for truth everywhere: in Great Britain, India (where he served as an officer in the Punjab Regiment), and Egypt (with the British Army.)

His search went on ceaselessly until an amazing epiphany in the Cotswold village where he was living (That event – on 5th May 1955 – provided the title for his first book, "5:5:55"). From that moment, everything changed: constant despair turned to joy, a duodenal ulcer disappeared instantly and 30-a-day smoking habit ceased effortlessly. But contact with traditional churches led to early disillusionment with organised religion and a longing to see people living in freedom from control.

Faith and spirituality without the shackles of religion – that was a popular theme in the 1960s, following years of monotonous austerity after the second World War – so Maurice's faith blossomed within a new kind of Christianity. He became a prominent leader in the Charismatic and House Church movements and was much in demand as a speaker in churches, house-groups, large public meetings and on radio. But, fame never appealed to him so, when the movement dissolved into a range of new denominations, Maurice continued his pursuit for truth – whatever the cost.

Printed in Poland
by Amazon Fulfillment
Poland Sp. z o.o., Wrocław